BACH FOR FLUTE

Bach

THAT'S EASY!™

Wise Publications
London/New York/Paris/Sydney/Copenhagen/Madrid

Exclusive Distributors:
Music Sales Limited
8/9 Frith Street, London W1V 5TZ, England.
Music Sales Pty Limited
120 Rothschild Avenue,
Rosebery, NSW 2018, Australia.

This book © Copyright 1994 by
Wise Publications
Order No. AM91872
ISBN 0-7119-3984-5

Music processed by Interactive Sciences Limited, Gloucester
Designed by Hutton & Partners

Music Sales' complete catalogue describes thousands of titles and is available in full colour sections by subject, direct from
Music Sales Limited. Please state your areas of interest and send a cheque/postal order for £1.50 for postage to:
Music Sales Limited, Newmarket Road, Bury St. Edmunds, Suffolk IP33 3YB.

CONTENTS

Air
from Suite in F

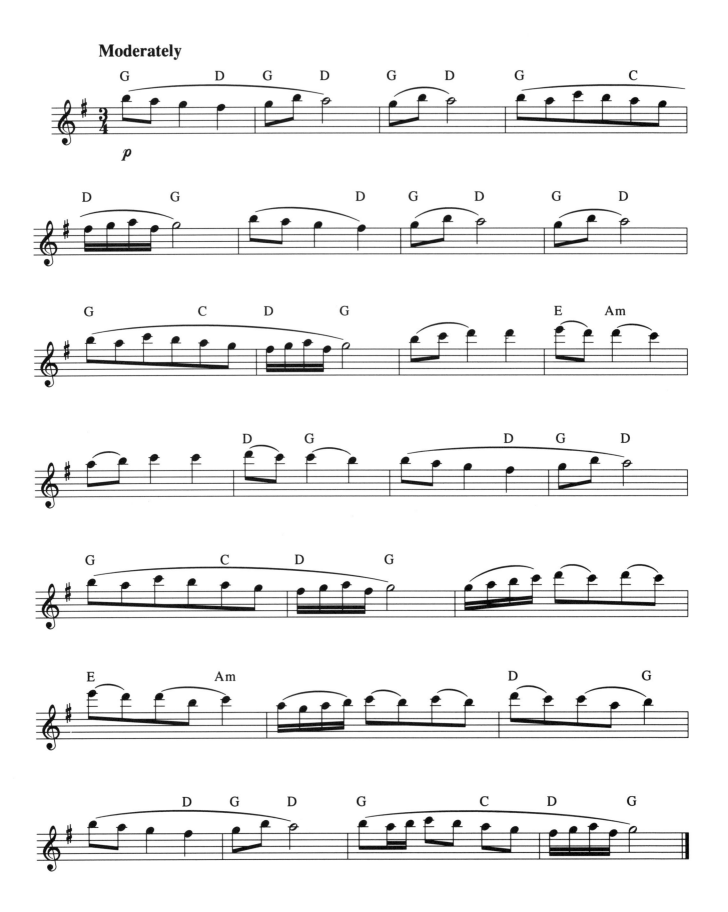

Air
from The Peasant Cantata

Air in D Major
from Orchestral Suite in D

Slow

Aria

Badinerie
from Orchestral Suite in B minor

Bourrée

Bourrée No. 1
from French Overture

Bourrée No. 1
from Orchestral Suite in C

Bright

Come Sweetest Death, Come, Blessed Rest

In Tears Of Grief
from St Matthew Passion

Moderately

Jesu, Joy Of Man's Desiring

With easy movement

Lie Still, O Sacred Limbs
from St John Passion

Moderately

March

With movement

Minuet
from Orchestral Suite No. 2 in B Minor

Moderately

Minuet in C Minor

Moderately

Minuet in D Minor

Minuet in G

Minuet in G Minor

Musette

Passepied No. 1
from Orchestral Suite in C

Prelude in E Minor
from Eight Short Preludes & Fugues for Organ

Prepare Thyself, Zion
from Christmas Oratorio

With movement

Rinkart
from Kommt Seelen

Sarabande
from Cello Suite in E♭

Sarabande
from Sonata Nach Reincken

Moderately

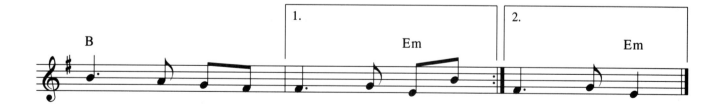

Sarabande
from Suite in E♭

Moderately

Sheep May Safely Graze

Moderately

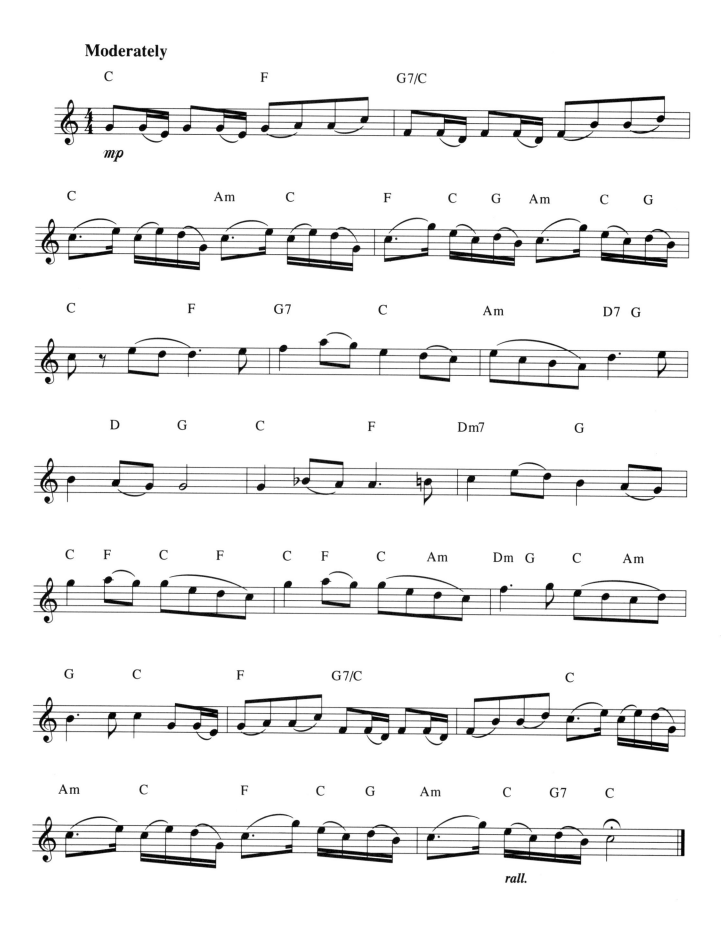

Sleepers, Wake! A Voice Is Calling

Moderately

rall.

BEETHOVEN

Wise Publications
London/New York/Paris/Sydney/Copenhagen/Madrid

Exclusive Distributors:
Music Sales Limited
8/9 Frith Street, London W1V 5TZ, England.

Music Sales Pty Limited
120 Rothschild Avenue,
Rosebery, NSW 2018, Australia.

Music Sales Corporation
257 Park Avenue South
New York, NY10010, United States of America.

This book © Copyright 1994 by
Wise Publications
Order No. AM91883
ISBN 0-7119-3999-3

Music processed by Interactive Sciences Limited, Gloucester
Designed by Hutton & Partners

Music Sales' complete catalogue describes thousands of titles and is available in full colour sections by subject, direct from
Music Sales Limited. Please state your areas of interest and send a cheque/postal order for £1.50 for postage to:
Music Sales Limited, Newmarket Road, Bury St. Edmunds, Suffolk IP33 3YB.

Printed in the United Kingdom by
Caligraving Limited, Thetford, Norfolk.

CONTENTS

Allegretto
from Sonata in E, Op.14, No.1

With movement

Bagatelle
Op.119, No.1

German Dance

Bright

Ländler

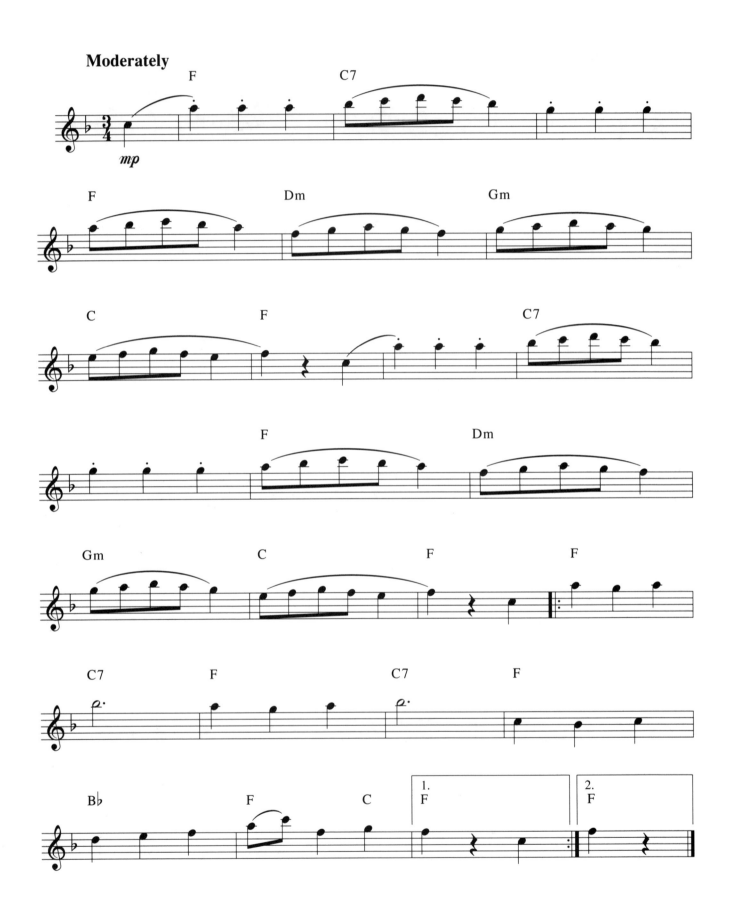

Minuet In G

Moderately

3rd Movement Theme
from Piano Concerto No.1 in C (Rondo) Op.15

2nd Movement Theme
from Piano Sonata (Pathétique) Op.13

Moderately

1st Movement Themes
from Piano Concerto No. 3 in C Minor, Op. 37

Moderately fast

2nd Movement Theme
from Piano Sonata, Op.14, No.2

1st Movement Theme
from Piano Sonata, Op. 26

Moderately

2nd Movement Theme
from Piano Sonata, Op. 90

Not too fast

Tempo di Menuetto
from Sonata in G, Op. 49, No. 2

Moderately

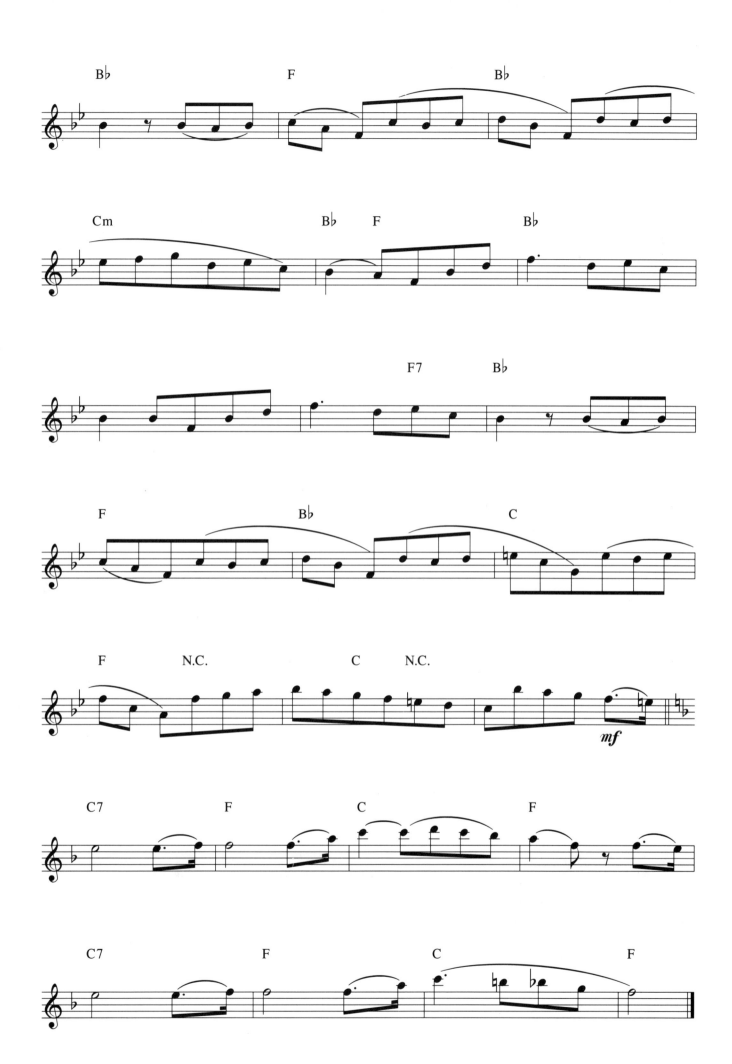

19

Slow Movement Theme
from Symphony No.5

Moderately

1st Movement Themes
from Symphony No.6 (Pastoral)

Not too fast

4th Movement Theme
from Symphony No.6 (Pastoral)

Moderately

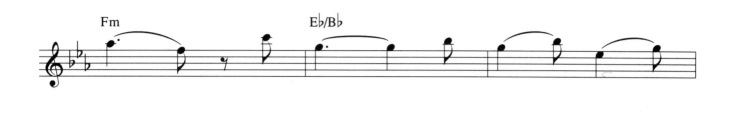

Song: Die Liebe Des Nächsten
(Brotherly Love)

2nd Movement Theme
from Symphony No.7

Last Movement Theme
from Symphony No. 9 (Ode To Joy)

With movement

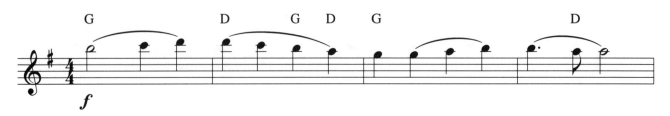

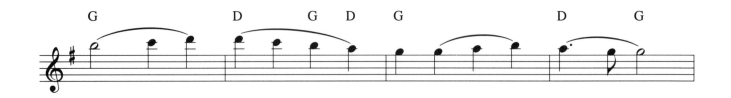

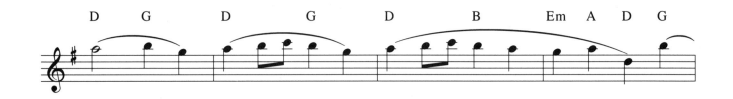

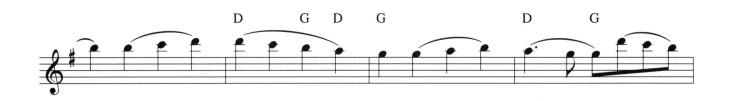

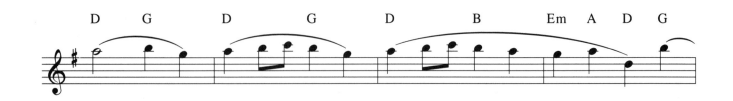

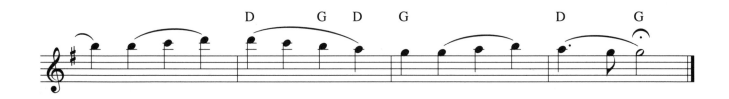

Theme from 2nd Movement of Serenade
Op. 25

Slow

Turkish March
from The Ruins Of Athens

Bright tempo

Two German Dances

HANDEL FOR FLUTE

HANDEL

Wise Publications
London/New York/Paris/Sydney/Copenhagen/Madrid

Exclusive Distributors:
Music Sales Limited
8/9 Frith Street,
London W1V 5TZ, England.

Music Sales Pty Limited
120 Rothschild Avenue,
Rosebery, NSW 2018, Australia.

Music Sales Corporation
257 Park Avenue South,
New York, NY10010, United States of America.

This book © Copyright 1994 by
Wise Publications
Order No. AM91887
ISBN 0-7119-4003-7

Music processed by Interactive Sciences Limited, Gloucester
Designed by Hutton & Partners

Music Sales' complete catalogue describes thousands of titles and is available in full colour sections by subject, direct from
Music Sales Limited. Please state your areas of interest and send a cheque/postal order for £1.50 for postage to:
Music Sales Limited, Newmarket Road, Bury St. Edmunds, Suffolk IP33 3YB.

CONTENTS

Air
from Water Music

Fairly slow

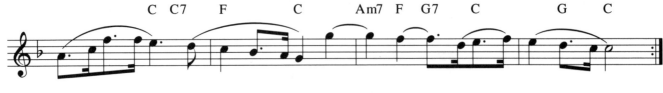

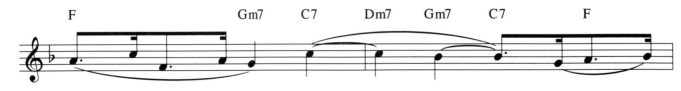

Bourrée
from Water Music

5

But Who May Abide
from Messiah

Moderately slow

Dance And Trio
from Amadigi di Gaula

Bright tempo

He Shall Feed His Flock
from Messiah

Moderately

Holy, Holy
from Redemption

9

Hornpipe
from Water Music

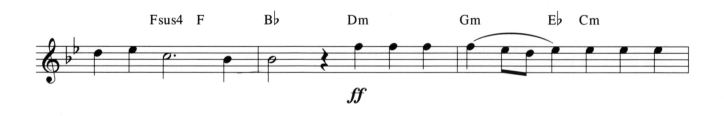

How Beautiful Are The Feet
from Messiah

Moderately slow

I Know That My Redeemer Liveth
from Messiah

Not too slow

Larghetto
from Concerto Grosso No. 12

Moderately

Largo
from Xerxes

Lascia Ch'io Pianga
from Rinaldo

Moderately

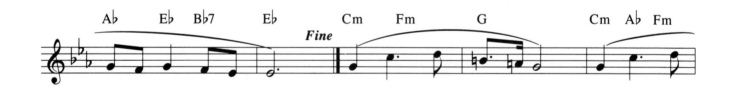

Let The Bright Seraphim
from Samson

With movement

Love In Her Eyes
from Acis and Galatea

March
from Scipione

With movement

Martial Movement
from Fireworks Music

Bright tempo

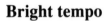

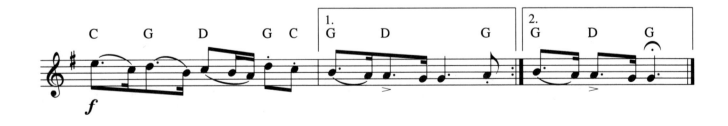

Minuet

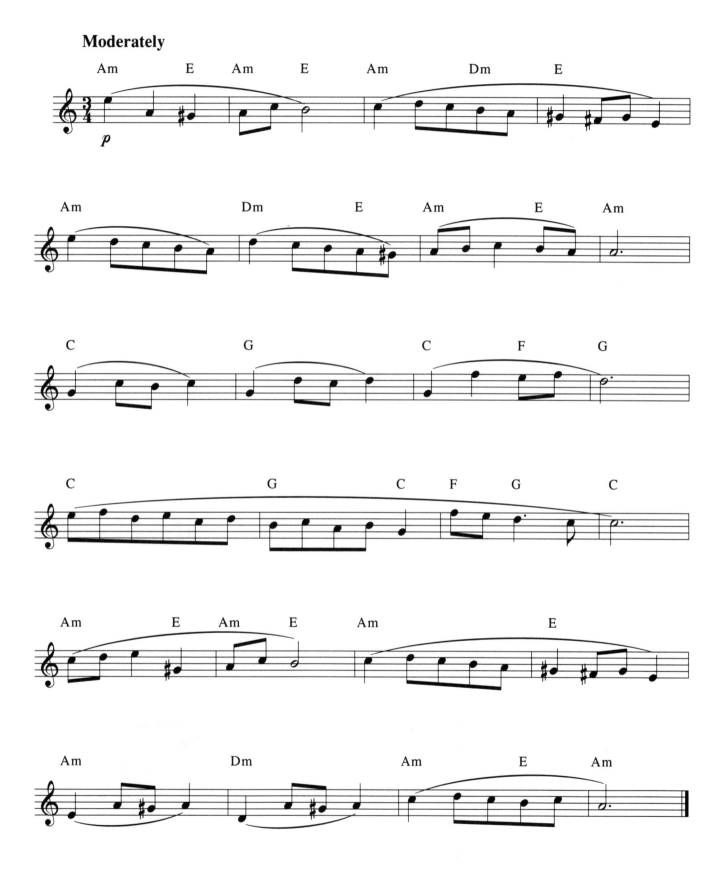

Minuet
from Berenice

O Lovely Peace
from Judas Maccabaeus

O Magnify The Lord
from Chandos Anthem No. 5

O Placido Il Mare
from Siroe

Sarabande
from Oboe Concerto No. 3 in G Minor

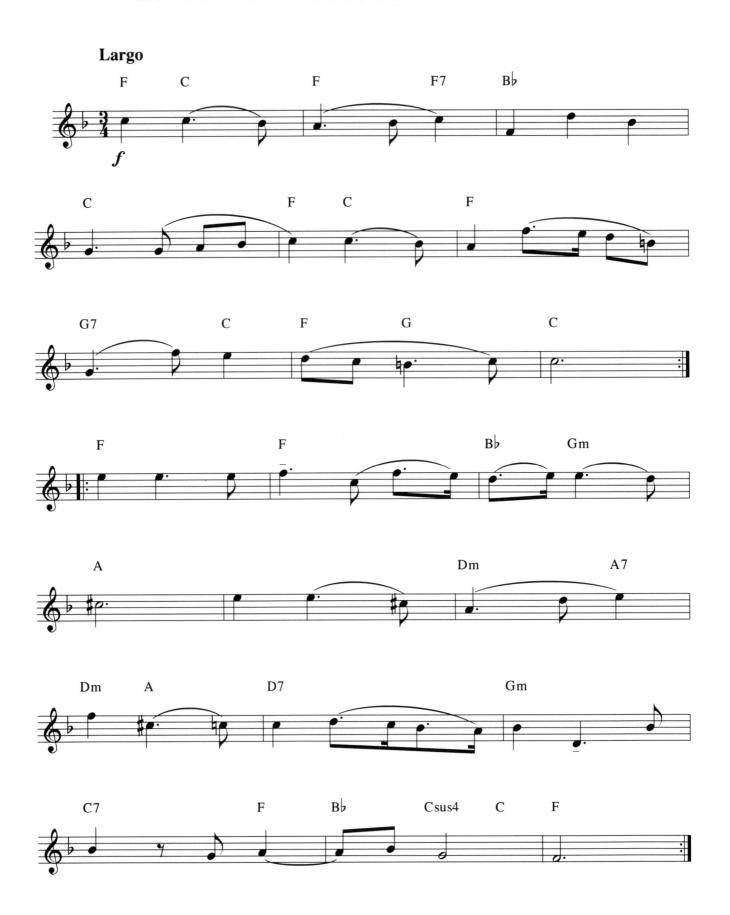

See The Conquering Hero Comes
from Judas Maccabaeus

Majestically

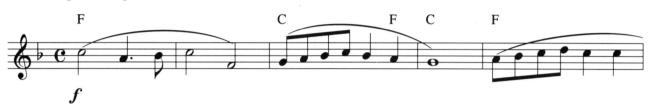

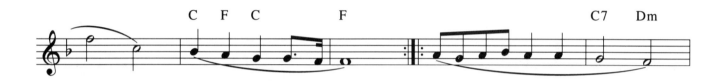

Silent Worship
from Ptolomy

Themes from Hallelujah Chorus
from Messiah

Bright tempo

Where E'er You Walk
from Semele

Moderately

Where Is This Stupendous Stranger
from Redemption

Moderately

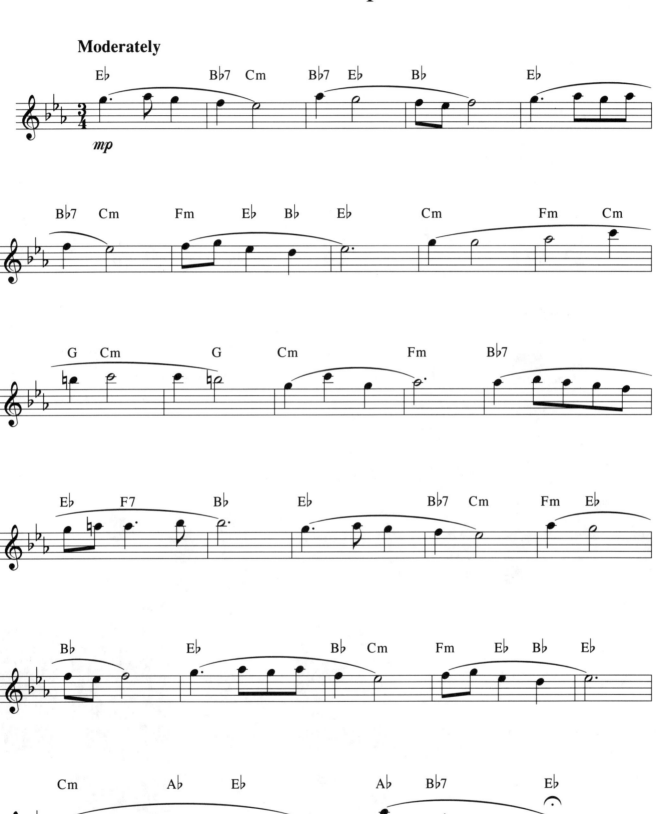

The Beatles

Enya

Phil Collins

Van Morrison

Bob Dylan

Sting

Paul Simon

Tracy Chapman

Eric Clapton

Pink Floyd

New Kids On The Block

Bryan Adams

Tina Turner

Elton John

Bee Gees

Whitney Houston

AC/DC

Bringing you the words

All the latest in rock and pop. Plus the brightest and best in West End show scores. Music books for every instrument under the sun. And exciting new teach-yourself ideas like "Let's Play Keyboard" - in cassette/book packs, or on video. Available from all good music shops.

and music

Music Sales' complete catalogue lists thousands of titles and is available free from your local music shop, or direct from Music Sales Limited. Please send a cheque or postal order for £1.50 (for postage) to:

Music Sales Limited
Newmarket Road,
Bury St Edmunds,
Suffolk IP33 3YB

Buddy

Five Guys Named Moe

Les Misérables

West Side Story

Phantom Of The Opera

Show Boat

The Rocky Horror Show

Bringing you the world's best music.

MOZART

Wise Publications
London/New York/Paris/Sydney/Copenhagen/Madrid

Exclusive Distributors:
Music Sales Limited
8/9 Frith Street, London W1V 5TZ, England.
Music Sales Pty Limited
120 Rothschild Avenue,
Rosebery, NSW 2018, Australia.

This book © Copyright 1994 by
Wise Publications
Order No. AM91876
ISBN 0-7119-3988-8

Music processed by Interactive Sciences Limited, Gloucester
Designed by Hutton & Partners

Music Sales' complete catalogue describes thousands of titles and is available in full colour sections by subject, direct from
Music Sales Limited. Please state your areas of interest and send a cheque/postal order for £1.50 for postage to:
Music Sales Limited, Newmarket Road, Bury St. Edmunds, Suffolk IP33 3YB.

Your Guarantee of Quality
As publishers, we strive to produce every book to the highest commercial standards.

The music has been freshly engraved and the book has been carefully designed to minimise
awkward page turns and to make playing from it a real pleasure.

Particular care has been given to specifying acid-free, neutral-sized paper made from pulps which have not been
elemental chlorine bleached. This pulp is from farmed sustainable forests and was produced with special regard for the
environment. Throughout, the printing and binding have been planned to ensure a sturdy, attractive publication
which should give years of enjoyment.

If your copy fails to meet our high standards, please inform us and we will gladly replace it.

Printed in the United Kingdom by
Caligraving Limited, Thetford, Norfolk.

CONTENTS

1st Movement Theme
Eine Kleine Nachtmusik
K. 525

Adagio Theme
from Concerto in A Major for Clarinet
K.V. 622

Andantino
from Divertimento No. 13 in F
K. 253

Moderately

Ave Verum Corpus

Là Ci Darem La Mano
(You'll Lay Your Hand In Mine)
from Don Giovanni

Moderately

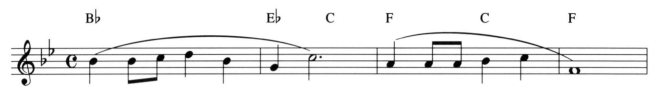

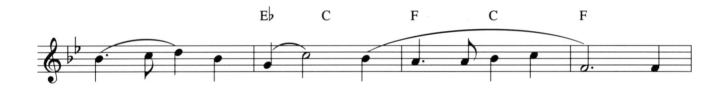

poco rit.

Elvira Madigan
Theme from Piano Concerto in C Major
K. 467

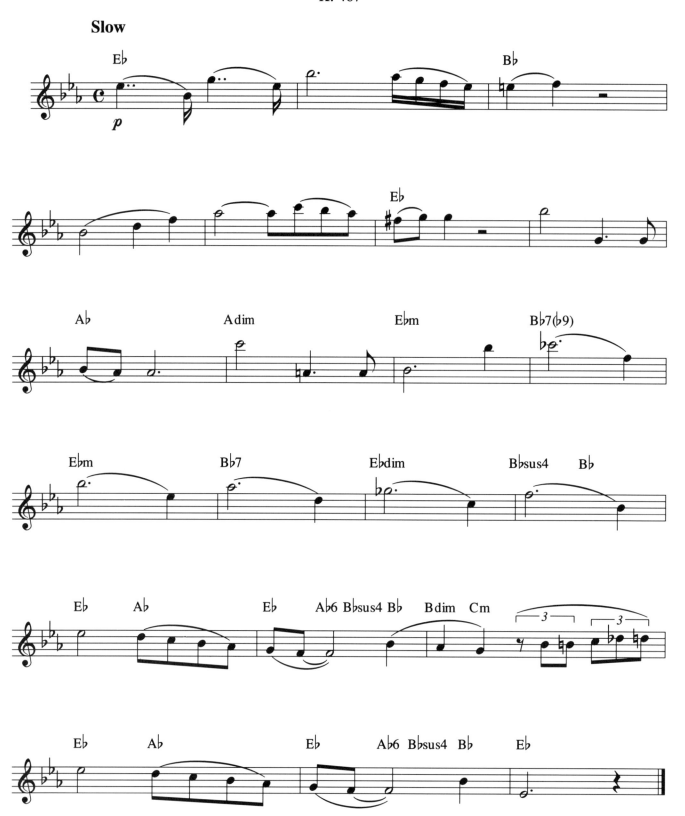

March Of The Priests
from The Magic Flute

Moderately

Minuet
from Sonata in E♭
K. 189

Minuet in F

K. 2

Moderately

Minuet in G

K. 315/a

Minuetto
from Eine Kleine Nachtmusik
K. 525

With movement

Minuetto Theme
from Haffner Symphony
K. 385

O Isis And Osiris
from The Magic Flute

Piano Concerto in B♭
Slow Movement
K. 450

Moderately

Romance
from Eine Kleine Nachtmusik
K. 525

Rondo Alla Turca
from Sonata in A
K. 300

With movement

Rondo Theme
from Violin Concerto in D Major
K. 211

Say Goodbye Now To Pastime
from The Marriage Of Figaro

Sonata in A
1st Movement Theme
K. 300

Moderately

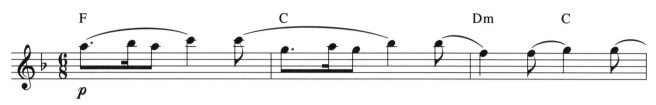

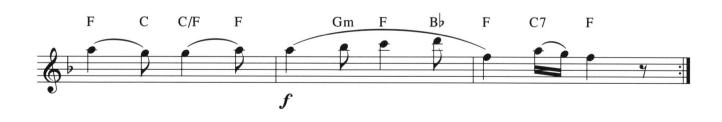

Sonata in C
2nd Movement Theme
K. 545

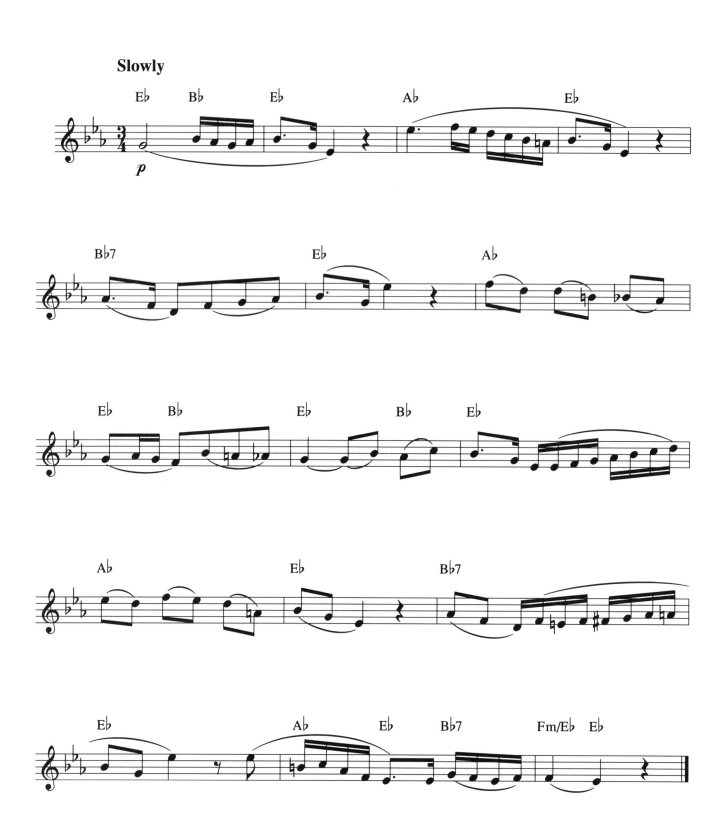

Sonata in C Minor
Last Movement Theme
K. 456

Bright

Song: "Lullaby"

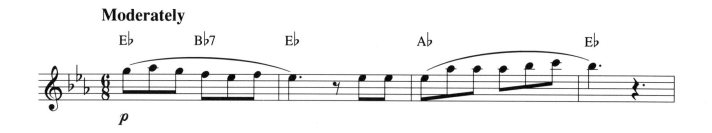

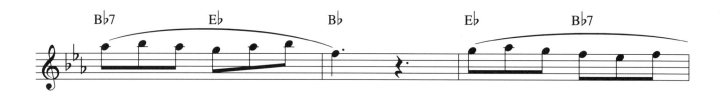

Song: "To Friendship"

Moderately

Tell Me Fair Ladies
from The Marriage Of Figaro

Moderately

The Manly Heart That Claims Our Duty

from The Magic Flute

Moderately

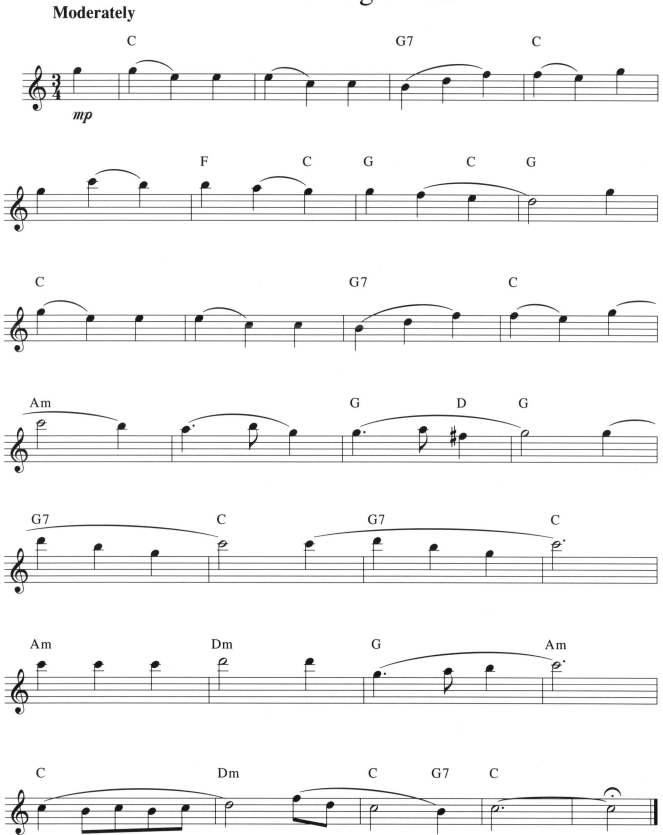

Theme from Symphony in G Minor

K. 550

With movement

Violin Sonata in E♭
Last Movement Theme
K. 481

With movement

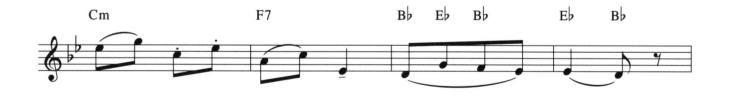
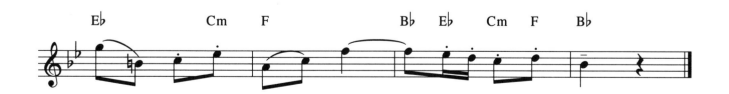

The Beatles
 Enya

 Phil Collins
 Van Morrison
 Bob Dylan

 Sting
 Paul Simon
 Tracy Chapman

Bringing you the
words

 Eric Clapton
 Pink Floyd
 New Kids On The Block

All the latest in rock and pop. Plus the brightest and best in West End show scores. Music books for every instrument under the sun. And exciting new teach-yourself ideas like "Let's Play Keyboard" - in cassette/book packs, or on video. Available from all good music shops.

 Bryan Adams
 Tina Turner
 Elton John

and
 Bee Gees
 Whitney Houston
 **AC/DC**

music

Music Sales' complete catalogue lists thousands of titles and is available free from your local music shop, or direct from Music Sales Limited. Please send a cheque or postal order for £1.50 (for postage) to:

Music Sales Limited
Newmarket Road,
Bury St Edmunds,
Suffolk IP33 3YB

 **Buddy**
 **Five Guys Named Moe**
 **Les Misérables**
 **West Side Story**

 **Phantom Of The Opera**
 **Show Boat**
 **The Rocky Horror Show**

**Bringing you the
world's best music.**

SYMPHONIC THEMES FOR FLUTE

Symphonic Themes

Wise Publications
London/New York/Paris/Sydney/Copenhagen/Madrid

Exclusive Distributors:
Music Sales Limited
8/9 Frith Street,
London W1V 5TZ, England.

Music Sales Pty Limited
120 Rothschild Avenue,
Rosebery, NSW 2018, Australia.

Music Sales Corporation
257 Park Avenue South,
New York, NY10010, United States of America.

This book © Copyright 1994 by
Wise Publications
Order No. AM91913
ISBN 0-7119-4029-0

Music processed by Interactive Sciences Limited, Gloucester
Designed by Hutton & Partners

Music Sales' complete catalogue describes thousands of titles and is available in full colour sections by subject, direct from
Music Sales Limited. Please state your areas of interest and send a cheque/postal order for £1.50 for postage to:
Music Sales Limited, Newmarket Road, Bury St. Edmunds, Suffolk IP33 3YB.

Printed in the United Kingdom by
Caligraving Limited, Thetford, Norfolk.

CONTENTS

Symphony No.2 in D
3rd Movement Theme

Composed by Ludwig van Beethoven (1770–1827)

Symphony No.6 (Pastoral)
3rd Movement Theme

Composed by Ludwig van Beethoven (1770–1827)

Symphony No.3 in E♭ (Eroica)
1st Movement Theme

Composed by Ludwig van Beethoven (1770–1827)

Symphony No.1 in C Minor
4th Movement Theme

Composed by Johannes Brahms (1833–1897)

Moderately

Symphony No.3 in F
3rd Movement Theme

Composed by Johannes Brahms (1833–1897)

Symphony No.9 in E Minor (From The New World)

2nd Movement Theme

Composed by Antonin Dvořák (1841–1904)

Symphony No.8 in G
3rd Movement Theme

Composed by Antonín Dvořák (1841–1904)

Symphony No.9 in E Minor
(From The New World)
Finale

Composed by Antonin Dvořák (1841–1904)

Symphony No.88 in G
Largo

Composed by Franz Joseph Haydn (1732–1809)

Symphony No.94 in G (Surprise)
2nd Movement Theme

Composed by Franz Joseph Haydn (1732–1809)

Symphony No.97 in C
2nd Movement Theme

Composed by Franz Joseph Haydn (1732–1809)

Not too slow

Symphony No.104 in D (London)
2nd Movement Theme

Composed by Franz Joseph Haydn (1732–1809)

Symphony No.3 (Scottish)
3rd Movement Theme

Composed by Felix Mendelssohn (1809–1847)

Moderately slow

Symphony No.4 (Italian)
2nd Movement Theme

Composed by Felix Mendelssohn (1809–1847)

Symphony No.4 (Italian)
3rd Movement Theme

Composed by Felix Mendelssohn (1809–1847)

With movement

Symphony No.6 in F
Minuet And Trio

Composed by Wolfgang Amadeus Mozart (1756–1791)

Symphony No.50 in D
2nd Movement Theme

Composed by Wolfgang Amadeus Mozart (1756–1791)

Symphony No.4 in C Minor
Andante

Composed by Franz Schubert (1797–1828)

Symphony No.5 in B♭
2nd Movement Theme

Composed by Franz Schubert (1797–1828)

Moderately

Symphony No.8 in B Minor (Unfinished)
1st Movement Theme

Composed by Franz Schubert (1797–1828)

Symphony No.5
Extract from Andante Cantabile

Composed by Piotr Ilyich Tchaikovsky (1840–1893)

Slowly and with feeling

Symphony No.6 (Pathétique)
March Theme

Composed by Piotr Ilyich Tchaikovsky (1840–1893)

Symphony No.6 (Pathétique)
1st Movement Theme

Composed by Piotr Ilyich Tchaikovsky (1840–1893)

Symphony No.6 (Pathétique)
2nd Movement Theme

Composed by Piotr Ilyich Tchaikovsky (1840–1893)